HOW DID DINOSAURS GET SO GIGANTIC?

A BOOK ABOUT DINOSAURS

written by
clayton tobias grider
illustrated by
srimalie bassani

The most famous and quite possibly our favorite animals from the past are dinosaurs! We see them all the time in movies, books, and games. Dinosaurs are everywhere! Ever since the first fossils were found, humans have been captivated by dinosaurs. Paleontologists (people who study fossils) work hard to decipher fossil records in order to figure out the mystery of the dinosaurs.

As you can imagine, creatures that existed millions of years ago do not leave a lot of clues, yet, hardworking paleontologists have managed to piece some important and interesting information together.

Scotty

One of the largest Tyrannosaurus rex fossils was discovered in Canada.

HOW DID DINOSAURS GET SO GIGANTIC?

Did they wear stilts in order to trick everyone into thinking they were huge?

Dinosaurs definitely didn't need stilts! The environment and the dinosaurs around them are what made them huge.

Yeah, they definitely walked on stilts... that's what I heard...

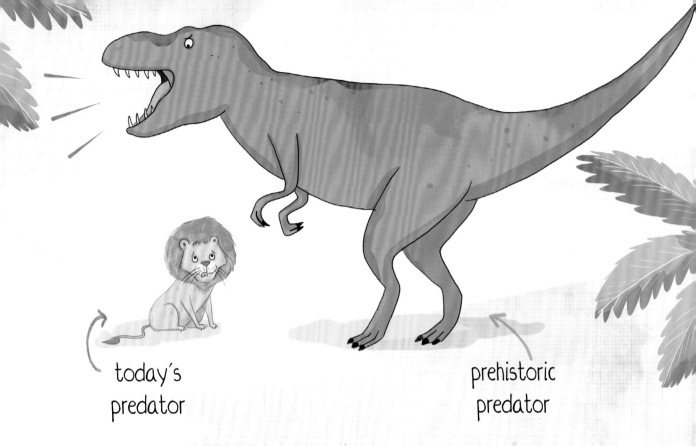

today's predator

prehistoric predator

An animal's size can vary for many different reasons. For example, giraffes are large because their long necks are what allow them to reach the tall trees that grow around them. Paleontologists used what they know about animals like giraffes to learn about dinosaurs too. *Brontosaurus* had long neck bones and small skulls, similar to giraffes. This led paleontologists to believe that *Brontosaurus* used its long neck to help it get food from tall trees as well.

Another reason that animals grow so big is to deter predators. If you are a lone lion and had to choose to go after a gazelle or an elephant, the smart choice would be to go after the smaller prey. This has a domino effect. Predators need to get bigger in order to be able to hunt. On Earth today, the largest land predator, the polar bear, can weigh on average 900 pounds (408 kilograms). In the dinosaur age, a theropod, like the *Tyrannosaurus rex*, could have weighed up to 15,500 pounds (7,030 kilograms)!

ELEPHANT VS BRONTOSAURUS

African Elephant

Brontosaurus

66 feet
(20 meters)

13 feet
(4 meters)

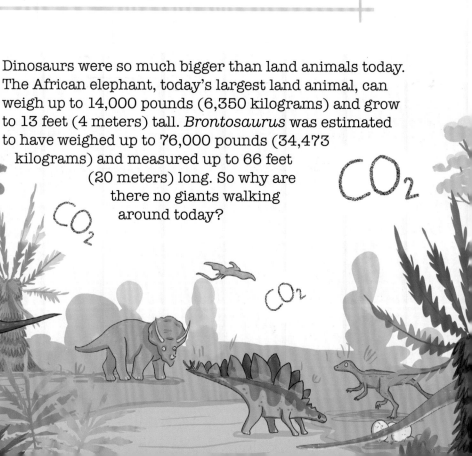

Dinosaurs were so much bigger than land animals today. The African elephant, today's largest land animal, can weigh up to 14,000 pounds (6,350 kilograms) and grow to 13 feet (4 meters) tall. *Brontosaurus* was estimated to have weighed up to 76,000 pounds (34,473 kilograms) and measured up to 66 feet (20 meters) long. So why are there no giants walking around today?

CO_2

CO_2

CO_2

There are many theories as to why that is the case. One of the theories is that there was an abundance of vegetation. The level of carbon dioxide in the sky back then was much higher than it is today. Carbon dioxide is important for plants to survive. This combined with higher world temperatures meant that plants grew in abundance. Dinosaurs were able to grow so big because of their access to so much food! Huge dinosaurs did not have to worry about setting some time away for basking in the sun like today's cold-blooded animals—they had a plant buffet!

Speaking of cold-blooded, another theory is that dinosaurs got so big in order to regulate their internal temperatures. Some paleontologists believe that giant plant-eating dinosaurs were cold-blooded, or animals that cannot keep a constant body temperature and rely on the environment to regulate their temperature. For these giant herbivore (plant-eating) dinosaurs, being so large would help regulate their internal temperatures.

HOW DID DINOSAURS LOOK?

Did they wear sweaters and have rainbow mohawks?

That would be a pretty cool, but in reality we don't know what exactly dinosaurs looked like back in the day. Material like feathers and skin rarely survive today, so our understanding of what they may have looked like has changed over the years.

Is it a horn or a thumb?

FULL IGUANODON SKELETON

For example, the earliest dinosaur models shown to the public made dinosaurs look like modern day iguanas. They had two legs on either side of their bodies (called splayed legs) and greenish, bumpy skin. Over time, paleontologists realized that most dinosaurs did not have splayed legs. They even realized that they put the bones of some dinosaurs in the wrong spot! When they were first putting the giant Iguanodon together, they thought it had a horn. But it was not a horn, it was a thumb!

Now it all makes sense.

Many times not all of the bones for a dinosaur are found in one place, meaning paleontologists had to put them together using information they already had or informed guesses. It wasn't until they discovered a full skeleton that they realized their mistake!

One of the biggest breakthroughs came when paleontologists discovered that not all dinosaurs had scaly brown or green skin. Originally they had modeled dinosaurs after snakes and lizards of our time. Most snakes and lizards with those colors use them to blend into their environment for protection from predators. But some dinosaurs were so big, they didn't need to blend into their environment.

Do you think that snake can see me?

Hadrosaurus

Paleontologists have since learned that
like some birds today, there were
dinosaurs that had bright feathers
and skin in order to attract other
mates. Dinosaurs that lived in herds
(like *Hadrosaurus*) may have had
unique skin patterns so they could
distinguish their herd members
from other herds. While some dinosaurs
did have earthy colors, the world of
dinosaurs was more colorful and
feathered than what was once believed.

HOW DO FOSSILS FORM?

Did people in the past bury animal bones to trick paleontologists today?

Fossils aren't put there by people! Bones or other fossilized matter were buried long ago. Over a long, long time, that material fossilized.

HOW A FOSSIL IS FORMED:

The ammonite dies and falls to the bottom of the sea. It is then absorbed by the sand. Over time, the minerals contained in the water transform the shell into stone.

Fossilization is never a sure thing and it is actually quite rare. That is why dinosaur bones are so hard to come by! The whole process takes a long time and needs the right conditions for it to occur. That is why finding fossils is a big deal.

Perfectly preserved Mammoth.

Sometimes not just the bones of dinosaurs are found. In some places, like the Arctic where it is extremely cold, flesh and hair and muscle can be preserved!

FOSSILS

FIVE MAIN TYPES OF FOSSILS

There are many different ways for fossils to form.

The first way is permineralization (that's a big word!). This is a process in which minerals move into the cells of plants and animals and crystallize (making it more like a rock). This is the most common type of fossil preservation. Teeth, bones, shells, and even wood can be crystallized. For wood, we call the fossils petrified material.

Petrified or Permineralization

Molds and Casts (Impression Fossils)

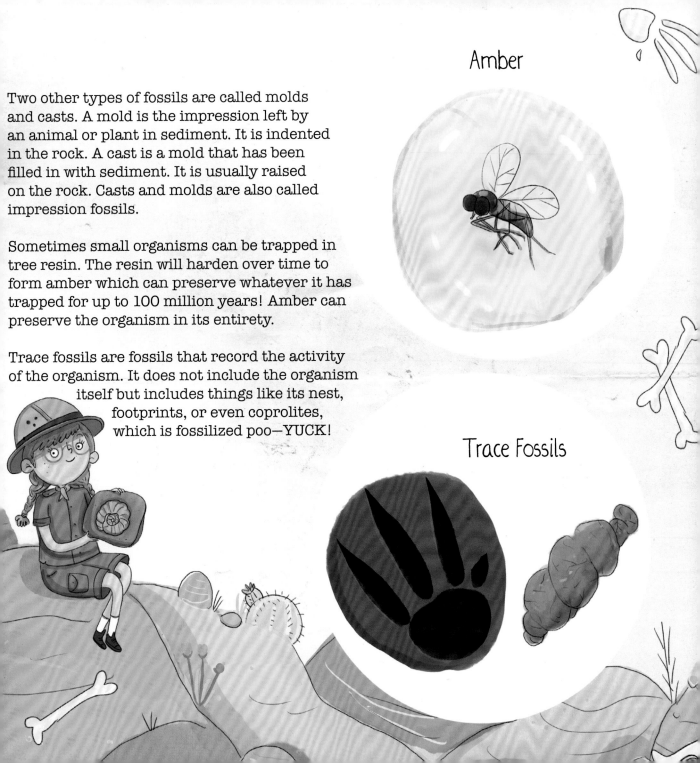

Two other types of fossils are called molds and casts. A mold is the impression left by an animal or plant in sediment. It is indented in the rock. A cast is a mold that has been filled in with sediment. It is usually raised on the rock. Casts and molds are also called impression fossils.

Sometimes small organisms can be trapped in tree resin. The resin will harden over time to form amber which can preserve whatever it has trapped for up to 100 million years! Amber can preserve the organism in its entirety.

Trace fossils are fossils that record the activity of the organism. It does not include the organism itself but includes things like its nest, footprints, or even coprolites, which is fossilized poo—YUCK!

Amber

Trace Fossils

HOW DID STEGOSAURUS MEET T. REX?

Did they go to a dino dance party together?

Actually, they never met because they lived during two completely different times in history!

FUN FACT:
Humans and the T. re[x] are closer on the world[] timeline than the T. rex and Stegosaurus!

Dino dance party!

Ammonite
↓
Paleozoic Era

252 Milli[on] Years Ag[o]

It is very common to lump all dinosaurs together into a single time period, but the entire era of dinosaurs (called the Mesozoic Era) extended from 251 million years ago to 65 million years ago! *Stegosaurus* roamed Earth during the late Jurassic Period between 159 and 144 million years ago. *Tyrannosaurus rex* lived during the late Cretaceous Period, about 90 to 65 million years ago. There was at least 54 million years between the times they were on Earth!

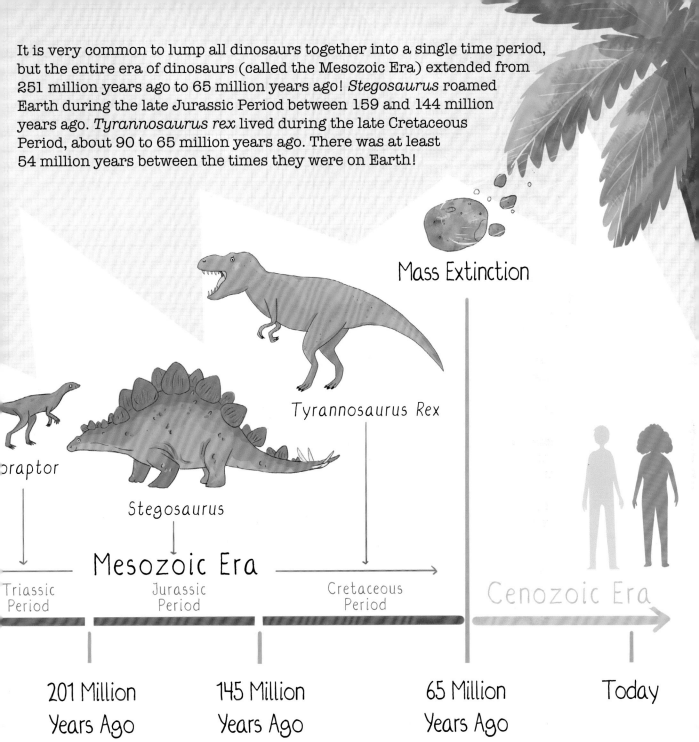

Mass Extinction

Tyrannosaurus Rex

raptor

Stegosaurus

Mesozoic Era

Cenozoic Era

Triassic Period	Jurassic Period	Cretaceous Period

201 Million Years Ago

145 Million Years Ago

65 Million Years Ago

Today

EARTH'S HISTORY

Earth's history can be broken down into four different spans of time. The first section, Precambrian, started 4.6 BILLION years ago! This was when Earth was formed. The next section was called the Paleozoic Era, which was from 538.8 million to 252 million years ago. This era started off with the Cambrian explosion which was a time period of rapid growth of life. The third era is called the Mesozoic Era and it was from 252 million to 65 million years ago. This was the era of the dinosaurs. The final era is called the Cenozoic Era. It began 65 million years ago and is the era we are living in now.

PRECAMBRIAN
4.6 billion years ago–
541 million years ago

PALEOZOIC ERA
538.8–252 million years ago

MESOZOIC ERA
252–65 million years ago

The dinosaur era, the Mesozoic Era, is broken down into three periods: the Triassic Period, Jurassic Period, and the Cretaceous Period. During each of these periods there were various types of wildlife and plant life.

The Triassic Period (252 million to 201 million years ago) was dominated by archosaurs on land and giant plesiosaurs in the oceans. The Jurassic Period (201 million to 145 million years ago) is the most famous period for dinosaurs. Dinosaurs such as the *Stegosaurus* and *Brachiosaurus* lived during this time. The final period was the Cretaceous Period (145 million to 65 million years ago). This warm period still had dinosaurs, such as *Velociraptor* and *Triceratops*, roaming the Earth, but other things, such as mammals and flowering plants, started to emerge.

CENOZOIC ERA
65 million years ago—present

HOW DID DINOSAURS DISAPPEAR?

Did they put on a magic show and do a very special dino disappearing act?

Dinosaurs didn't exactly disappear. There was what is called a mass extinction event.

This event was known as the K-T extinction event. It happened when an asteroid hit Earth causing 80 percent of all life on our planet to go extinct. The size of the asteroid was around 6 to 9 miles (10 to 15 kilometers) in diameter. It was HUGE!

comet

broken satellite

empty rocket

scrap metal

meteorites

Look at all that space debris!

The asteroid impacted the Yucatán Peninsula in Mexico. Huge clouds of dust and debris blotted out the sun. Since plants need the sun to make food, many plants began to die off. Soon the herbivores (animals that only eat plants) did not have enough food to eat. After the herbivores died, carnivores (animals that eat other animals) did not have enough food to eat. This is how dinosaurs as we know them became extinct.

Thankfully, large asteroids, like the one that killed the dinosaurs, are rare. Earth does get hit with space debris every year, an estimated 15,000 tons worth, but most of it is small and falls into the ocean without causing any harm.

HOW DO DINOSAURS WALK AMONG US?

Do dinosaurs get stuck in traffic to go to their day job?

No, and you would not want to come face to face with a living *Tyrannosaurus rex*, especially if he was late for work!

Only a small group of dinosaurs survived the giant asteroid that hit Earth. They did not look like the big dinosaurs that you think of when you picture dinosaurs. These smaller dinosaurs were able to survive by eating insects and other small prey. Some of them are still around today!

Corvus (Crow)

Caudipteryx

Protarchaeopteryx

Archaeopteryx

Eoalulavis

Sinosauropteryx

Velociraptor

Unenlagia

Archaeopteryx

Eoalulavis

Corvus
(Crow)

That's right! Birds evolved from theropod dinosaurs over 150 million years ago. Some dinosaurs developed feathers and small wings long before they gained the ability to fly. Why would an animal want wings when they could not fly?

Underdeveloped wings can still be useful! Looking at modern day examples, some ground birds are able to run up almost vertical surfaces without actually flying. Ducks use their wings to move faster over water and baby chicks use them like parachutes when falling from high heights.

Dinosaurs with Feathers
Fact or Fiction?

Dinosaurs and modern day birds share a number of similarities. Birds are bipedal (which means they walk on two legs). Theropod dinosaurs were bipedal, too! Some theropods even had feathers. In Australia, paleontologists have found feather fossils and shown that they were used to help dinosaurs survive in cold climates. Another characteristic that theropods share with birds is that they had three forward facing toes and a small backward-facing one.

We may not have giant dinosaurs wandering around, but it is pretty cool to know we live among their modern ancestors.

DINO PENCIL HOLDER

Need something to guard your pencils? Try making a dino pencil holder!

What you need:

- 4 toilet paper rolls
- paint
  (choose any color you like)
- paintbrush
- stapler
- 1 piece of construction paper
  (choose any color you like)
- markers or colored pencils
- glue
- googly eyes
  (optional)
- scissors

Directions:

1. Paint your toilet paper rolls whatever color you like then set aside to dry. Depending on the type of paint, you may need to repeat this step.

2. Once dry, use a stapler to connect the rolls together with two in front and two in back.

3. Draw a long neck and tail (see photo) on your construction paper. Draw a mouth and eyes or glue on googly eyes to either side of the head.

4. Carefully cut out the neck and tail pieces with scissors.

5. Glue your neck and tail to either end of the group of toilet paper rolls. Apply a small amount of glue to both sides of the back of the tail and the back of the neck. Then place the sides with glue between the toilet paper rolls (see photo).

6. Place your pens and pencils in your pencil holder!

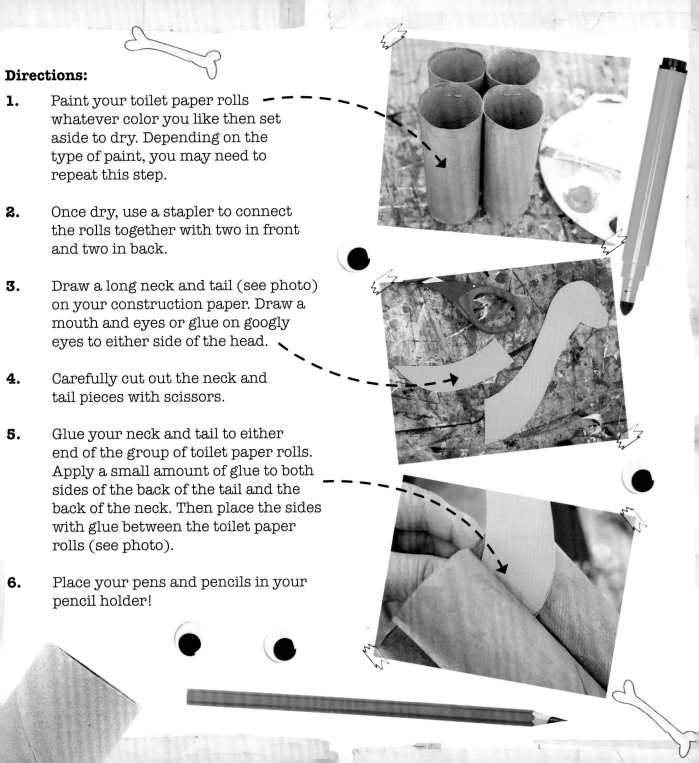

DINOSAUR FOSSIL COOKIES

Make your very own fossils that you can eat following these simple instructions. Be sure to ask an adult for help and permission before doing this activity.

What you need:

- 2 3/4 cups all-purpose flour
- 1 tsp baking soda
- 1/2 tsp baking powder
- 1 cup unsalted butter, softened
- 1 1/2 cups granulated sugar
- 1 large egg
- 1 tsp vanilla extract
- Circular cookie cutter or lid
- Small plastic dinosaur toys
  (Make sure they are clean!)

Directions:

1. Preheat your oven to 375°F (190°C). **(Be sure to ask an adult for help when using an oven!)**

2. In a medium bowl, whisk together the flour, baking soda, and baking powder. Set aside.

3. In a large bowl, cream together the softened butter and sugar until light and fluffy. Add the egg and vanilla extract, mixing well.

4. Gradually add the dry ingredients to the wet ingredients, mixing until the dough comes together.

5. Divide the dough into two equal parts. Roll out each portion on a floured surface to about 1/4-inch (.6 cm) thickness. Use a cookie cutter or a round lid to make circular cutouts.

6. Place the circular cookie dough on a parchment-lined baking sheet.

7. Bake in the preheated oven for 8–10 minutes or until the edges are lightly golden.

8. Once you pull out the cookies, carefully use your plastic toys to make imprints in your cookies. Those will be your fossils! Be sure to press hard enough to make an imprint but not too hard to break the cookie.

9. Let cool and then enjoy your fossil cookies!

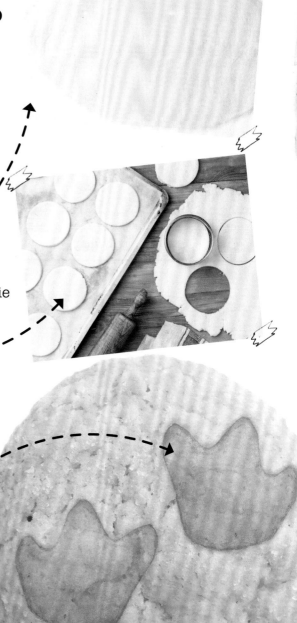

GLOSSARY

Asteroid – a big rock that floats in space; the cause of the K-T Extinction

Amber – a shiny, yellow-brown substance formed from tree resin that can sometimes trap insects inside

Carnivore – an animal that eats other animals

Carbon Dioxide – a gas that we breathe out and plants use for photosynthesis

Cast – a type of impression fossil in which only the shape of the organism can be seen

Coprolites – fossilized poo

Cold-blooded – animals that can't regulate their body temperature like humans can

Dinosaurs – prehistoric reptiles that lived on earth a long time ago

Fossil – the remains of a plant or animal from a long time ago

Fossilization – when something becomes a fossil over a long period of time

Herd – a group of animals that live together

Herbivores – animals that only eat plants

Impression Fossil – a fossil that shows the shape of an ancient plant or animal

K-T Extinction – a time when many dinosaurs and other animals disappeared

Mass Extinction Event – when many animals and plants die out all at once

Mold – a type of impression fossil in which the space of the fossil is filled with minerals

Paleontologist – a scientist who studies fossils

Permineralization – when minerals replace the parts of a plant or animal and make it hard like a rock

Predator – an animal that hunts and eats other animals

Theropod – a kind of meat-eating dinosaur

Trace Fossil – marks or signs left by ancient animals, like footprints

Tree Resin – sticky substance that comes from trees and can trap insects

Vegetation – plants and trees that grow in an area